EIGHT POWERFUL PRINCIPLES TO PROPEL YOUR PROJECT

PART 1

BY

APOSTLE DR. RAFAEL OSORIO

OCTOBER 2011

EDITORIAL RENOVACIÓN

SPRINGFIELD, MASSACHUSETTS

8 Powerful Principles To Propel Your Project

Part 1

By: Dr. Rafael Osorio

Published by:

Editorial Renovación
Springfield, MA 01105
All Rights Reserved

First Edition.
Copyright © 2011 by Dr. Rafael Osorio

ISBN 978-0-9841009-2-7 (English)
ISBN 978-0-9841009-1-0 (Spanish)
Printed in the United States of America

CONTENTS

DEDICATION

My wife, Loyda, and I would like to dedicate this book to our four children: Idaelis and her husband Lemuel, Rafael Luis and his wife Chaquira, and our two granddaughters, Kiana Liz and Victoria Eunice (Vicky). They are now the new generation, but they are still our projects. Every day we pray, teach, impart, and invest in their lives so that the full potential God has given them is manifested, and in turn, they are able to realize the projects God has designed for them.

We also dedicate the book to my brother, Luis A. Osorio, a musician and evangelist of the Lord for over 34 years. When the Lord called me into the ministry, I was leading an evangelistic musical group, of which my brother was a part. Then, upon entering the pastoral ministry in 1979, I transferred that project over to my brother. From that day until today, my brother has directed that Evangelistic Music Ministry (now called Creation Ministry) which travels throughout the island of Puerto Rico and to different nations. My brother Luis has been an example of perseverance, commitment, and dedication across many years in favor of a project. Brother, thank you for knowing how to promote this project through time. To God be the glory. Amen.

Acknowledgements

To the personnel of Editorial Renovación, namely Pastors Misael Ramos and Olga Suarez who were responsible for reviewing and editing the original manuscript in Spanish. Thank you for investing your time and, as always, for doing an excellent work. To Lemuel Gonzalez and Wilhem Morales, who were in charge of the art and cover designs. Thanks for placing your technological skills at the service of the Kingdom, and for making difficult things look easy.

To the prophet Isidra de Orbe in the Dominican Republic, who has covered this project in prayer throughout the entire process, and who even now remains standing in the gap in support of the project; now that it has entered the phase where it reaches the hands of our readers. In fact, I wrote the first seven principles while at her home in San Cristóbal, Dominican Republic.

I also recognize two businessmen of the International Apostolic Renewal Network, Santiago (Tito) Molina and Melvin Joel Galí, for investing financially in this project. Your sowing will release an even greater harvest in different areas. To all of these people, I bless you. Amen.

I would also like to thank the translation team for this edition. My sincerest gratitude to Lemuel Gonzalez (editor) and to the team: Rafael Luis Osorio, Lisandra Gonzalez, Gina Alicea, and Oldelis Ramos.

Apostle Dr. Rafael Osorio, President RIAR and
Senior Pastor IAR Springfield, MA, United States

Introduction

This book is based on two important premises. The first is that the reader has major projects that are beating strongly in his heart, and he is committed to bringing them to fruition throughout his life.

It is possible, for various reasons, that some of the readers are in a state of inaction, discouragement, or frustration about their projects. It is my prayer that by reading this book their passion for these projects re-awaken and that they might resume management of these projects and be encouraged to complete them.

The second premise is that the realization of any project will not happen automatically, as Tommy Newberry says in his book, <u>Success is not an accident</u>. This is why I share, directly, clearly, and concisely, eight principles that will help those who want to propel their project. Knowing and activating these eight principles will certainly help any project come out of the dream stage and advance every day.

In fact, this book is the first of a series of three, where I intend to share more simple but powerful principles, to promote your projects and achieve your full potential.

I came to understand the priority of these eight principles through my research on each one of them. Each principle tells you that if they are ignored, you will not be able to fulfill your project. The reality is that no one principle is more important than the other. Rather, the activation of all these principles together will have the effect of fueling and promoting your project.

A good way to maximize the teaching of this book at a church level or in groups is as follows. First, have each participant read the book chapter by chapter and answer the questions at the end of each chapter. The pastor or leader should then preach and teach a principle each week. We recommend a series of messages over eight Sundays. Then, each week the church is divided into small groups with a leader facilitating discussion on the teachings of the pastor and on the answers to the questions for each chapter. At the end of the eight chapters, we recommend a closing event where there is a review of the book, testimonies are shared, and a celebration is held including prayer for each person and their project.

I would love to hear about how this book helped you carry out your projects. You can send your responses to e-mail: 8Principles@IAR.cc.

Now I invite you to read the book so you can propel your project. It is time to get to work! Let us get down to business!

1ˢᵀ POWERFUL PRINCIPLE: INFORMATION

The principle that combats ignorance

My people are destroyed for lack of knowledge.
Hosea 4:6

Propelling your project requires you to be a well-informed person with access to valuable and relevant information. People with valuable information will have an advantage over people who live or operate in ignorance. The prophet Hosea wrote that God's people are destroyed for lack of knowledge (Hosea 4:6). Ignorance causes delay, blindness, limitation, and death. No one can progress in life living in ignorance. You cannot maximize what you do not know. "Ignorance is expensive ... It costs to be uninformed or even under-informed." [1] There may be prizes, rewards, blessings, connections, open doors, or huge opportunities available to you, but if you do not know about them then it would be as if they had not even existed.

It is not lack of opportunity that has many stagnant; but rather their lack of information.

Your project needs you to be an informed, intelligent, and wise person. The experts in this area distinguish between information or knowledge, intelligence, and wisdom.

- Knowledge: Information and data in different areas
- Intelligence: Ability to understand the knowledge that is being received
- Wisdom: The ability to effectively apply what is known and what is understood [2]

There are people who lack valuable information and live in complete ignorance. Others have information, but the information is irrelevant to their project. Some receive misleading or false information. In contrast, others have real but limited information and only a smaller group of people have access to real, valuable, and relevant information, and then maximize it. Which group are you in?

The healing of the paralytic at Capernaum is a great story, where Jesus is the main character, as he gave the order for this man's feet to return to normal (Mark 2:1-12). Nevertheless, for this miracle to come to pass, the paralytic had to activate at least four powerful spiritual principles. Here are the first three:

- He activated the principle of faith: "When Jesus saw their faith..." (v. 5)
- He activated the principle of strategy: They decided to climb to the roof, break through the roof, and lower the man before Jesus (v. 4)
- He turned on the principle of partnership: He found four friends who carried him to the place of action, and climbed to the roof (see v. 3)

The fourth principle we see in this passage is that of information. Though its listed last here, it is in fact the first principle the paralytic activates. Verse 1 says that they "heard He was in the house." When the paralytic learns that Jesus was near his house, healing, and teaching, he decides to make his way there. Without this valuable information, the paralytic would have missed this divine appointment, and in so doing, would have lost his miracle. Jesus was available, but without this knowledge, the miracle would not have taken place.

I ask you: what things do you need to know about your project to propel it towards its realization? What are the things that you do not know that are halting your project? Abraham was able to rescue Lot and his family from the rival kings, because he was informed that they had been taken hostage (Genesis 14:13-16). Likewise, Abraham was able to intercede for Lot in time because he received first-hand information (from God himself) concerning the divine judgment Sodom and Gomorrah were to going experience (Genesis 18:20-33). This valuable information enabled him to intercede on behalf of Lot and save his life. This shows the importance of information.

We need information and knowledge throughout our lives to move forward and realize our dreams and visions. Review the following vital areas where we need to have valuable information. Compare them against the biblical foundation.

- Identity: Who are you now that you are in Christ? 2 Cor. 5:17
- Potential: What are your gifts and abilities? 2 Cor. 1:12
- Assignment: What is the plan of God for your life? Jer. 29:11
- People: What people has God separated for you? Acts 9:17

3

- Season: In what season are you living? Phil. 4:11-12
- Finances: How do you manage and invest your money? 1 Peter 4:10
- Machinations: What are the enemy's weapons of choice against you? 2 Cor. 2:11
- Places: What is the place of your blessings? 1 Kings 17:8-9
- Decisions: How do you make better decisions? Acts 16:8-10
- Prayer: What will you ask for, and for what things will you intercede? James 4:3

It is sad to live in the information age where access is easy, fast, and inexpensive, and yet there are so many people with negative, inaccurate, limited, and even irrelevant information. Many have access to social sources such as Twitter, Facebook, cell phones, and cable, and still they are poorly informed. They use those sources to gossip, for entertainment, virtual games, sex, soap operas, etc. They only receive junk, irrelevant, superficial, frivolous, harmful, malicious, and even illegal information.

The enemy seeks to fill your ears and your mind with that junk information to prevent you from having access to powerful information that can bless and encourage your life and propel your project. Most likely, in order to start receiving good information, you must first clean out your "hard drive." You will have to "delete" many programs from your mind that set you back, pollute, and make you sick. You will need to enter into a process of renewal of your mind according to Romans 12:2.

The word of God is clear in stating that we are what we think. If the information stored in our mind is limited, negative, harmful, and trivial, then that is how we will be. You should not be surprised if your project has halted and is dying due to the poor and outdated information you have accumulated. It is time to find valuable information!

I worry about the lack of interest and effort in many children of God to learn and grow; they are reluctant to return to school, to take courses and attend seminaries, even those held in the church itself. For example, a course on good stewardship is offered in the church for a month, or in six sessions, and you see how they go missing from most classes, arrive late, sit in the back, fall asleep, fail to do the assignments, and so on. However, those same people can easily sit three to six hours in front of the TV and watch garbage. Check out their latest text messages, e-mails, and Facebook to see the depth of the content. Ask them what other books they are reading besides the Bible (assuming they are actually reading it).

Unfortunately, many have brain atrophy from lack of use or stimulus that challenges them to produce great things. I agree with what the prophetess Cindy Trimm says regarding information: "Information makes us responsible to implement what we already know. That's why many prefer to hide in ignorance, to avoid taking responsibility for their lives." [3]

There are things that God wants to reveal to their children through the Holy Spirit. This is the message of 1 Corinthians 2:9-10. However, the natural and carnal man cannot understand the things of God, because they are spiritually judged, but we can now come to know what God has given us through the Holy Spirit (1 Cor. 2:12-15).

The apostle Paul prayed that believers in the church at Colossae be filled with the knowledge of God's will in all wisdom and spiritual understanding (Colossians 1:9-10). God's children not only need information and natural intelligence, they also need wisdom and spiritual understanding. For us, the children of God, the need is even greater. How do we intend to be the head and not tail, conquer and govern cities, if our mind is full of worms: of silly and trivial things? The prophet Daniel was smarter and wiser than the wise men of his time; he was ten times greater than the rest (Daniel 1:17-20). The psalmist also declares that his wisdom and spiritual understanding exceeded that of his enemies, teachers, and even the elders (Psalm 119:98-100).

Paul lists some of the benefits of walking in spiritual wisdom and understanding, including: walking worthy of the Lord, pleasing him in all things, bearing fruit (e.g., producing results, and not being sterile or unproductive) in every good work and grow in the knowledge of God (e.g., growth, expansion, development of the potential). It is worth being an informed person, with knowledge and wisdom. Your project will advance more, if it is directed by a person with wisdom and spiritual understanding.

We should claim that anointing of wisdom and knowledge. The apostle James, just as the apostle Paul, believed in the importance of having classified information. He expected that every believer would have wisdom like Daniel.

> "If any of you lacks wisdom, let him ask of God, who gives to all liberally and without reproach, and it will be given to him."
>
> James 1:5

You need the wisdom of God to benefit from all the information you receive. Do you long to have such wisdom? Have you prayed to God for wisdom for your life and your project? God is the first one who desires to give us wisdom, and in abundance, but there needs to be someone who wants and values wisdom. Ask for that wisdom right now.

Your project requires you to be like the paralytic man in Capernaum; your project requires that you get accurate information to help you be present in your divine appointment, and not miss the blessing that is reserved for you. Remember: your project requires valuable and relevant information, and expects you to be a person full of intelligence and spiritual wisdom. Ignorance is expensive.

Notes

1) TD Jakes, <u>Before You Do: Making Great Decisions That You Won't Regret</u>, p. 9
2) Tommy Moya, <u>Destined for the heights</u>, p. 42-43
3) Cindy Trimm, Participation in the <u>Praise The Lord</u>, TV program on Sep 1, 2011.

Guiding Questions - Chapter One

1) Write the principle established in Hosea 4:6. Why is ignorance expensive?
2) Explain the author's quote: "It is not lack of opportunity that has many stagnant; but rather their lack of information."
3) Why is it important to have valuable and accurate information to propel your project forward?
4) What is the difference between knowledge, intelligence, and wisdom?
5) List the 10 vital areas where you should be well informed to promote your projects. Explain.

6) Name one of the things the Holy Spirit wants to do with the children of God according to 1 Cor. 2:12-15. What does this mean for you?

7) Write the prayer Paul made in favor of the Christians in Colossae. Do you think this prayer is still important?

8) What advantage does the person with spiritual intelligence have on others? Consider Col. 1:9-11.

9) What is the promise of James 1:5 as it relates to the subject we are studying?

10) How is the application of the truth of James 1:5 shown in the life of young Daniel (the prophet)? (See Daniel 1:17-20)

2ND POWERFUL PRINCIPLE: TIME

*The principle that recognizes that all
things have their appointed time*

To everything there is a season, a time for
every purpose under heaven
Ecclesiastes 3:1

Your project needs to recognize the importance of the resource called time, and how to maximize it. The success and effectiveness of your project are closely linked to time. If the principle of Ecclesiastes 3:1 is true, that to everything there is a season and everything that is desired under heaven has its time, then time management is vital to the success of your project. Identifying the season for each thing is mandatory before their fulfillment. It is not enough for the action to be good; it has to be executed at the right season and time to be effective.

**Good things done out of season run the risk
of being unproductive.**

Tommy Newberry says of the time factor in his book **Success Is Not an Accident: Change Your Choices; Change Your Life**:

- Success in life comes from one thing: deciding exactly what you want to accomplish and then deliberately choosing to invest the minutes and hours of your life doing only those things that move you in the direction of your goals.

- No matter who you are, your progress and success in life will depend, more than any other factor, on how you invest the twenty-four hours you're blessed with each day

- If you do not make the most out of an hour or even a minute, you'll never get a second chance. [1]

Mike Murdock in his book **The Law of Recognition**, says about the principle of time:

- Anything significant in your life will require the investment of time.

- Time has the same power. Some men use Time to create $10. Others do something different that hour and create $3,000.

- Recognition of the miracle gift of time will multiply your productivity, increase your financial worth and make every moment of relationships more valued. [2]

Time, unlike money, cannot be accumulated or saved for future use. Time is a unique resource: invisible, unchangeable, and unstoppable. That is the message of Ephesians 5:16 (HCSB): "Making the most of the time, because the days are evil." Put simply, time is either used or wasted. Time that has passed will not return. Are you making the most of your time? Do you value every year, every month, every week, every day, every hour? The psalmist declared: "This is the day the LORD has made; we will rejoice and be glad in it." (Psalm 118:24). Maximizing time begins by recognizing that every day we live is a gift from God, valuable and unique. Each day

2ND POWERFUL PRINCIPLE: TIME

should be used to learn something, review something, invest, love, appreciate, work, etc. Are you maximizing each day?

The Psalmist prayed to God to teach him to number his days so that he would develop wisdom in his heart (Psalm 90:12). Simply said, the psalmist recognizes the value of time, and his need to use it well. Do you pray to God for wisdom to maximize your money, resources, efforts, skills, and above all your time?

I am sure you have heard this excuse: if only I had more time, then I would do this and that, and start this or end that other thing. The problem we have is not a matter of needing more time, but of knowing how to take advantage of the time we already have. If 24 hours a day and seven days a week is not enough, then believe me that a 48-hour day and a 10-day week will not be enough either. You and I must live on 86,400 seconds, 1,440 minutes or 24 hours each day. [3]

Some people have dreams, visions, and big projects, but days and months go by and they do nothing in favor of them; they do not even have a plan. They are dominated by laziness, slumber, and inaction. They waste time on trivial things. People who will complete their project have a schedule to manage their time. They organize each week, decide the things they have to do, why they are to do them, and give those things a day and a time. These people have clear priorities in life; they know what is truly important and what is secondary. Can you name the top five priorities in your life, how they are arranged, and how much time you spend in each? As stated by Newberry: "There is always enough time to achieve what God wants you to accomplish." [4]

Many children of God live disorganized! They arrive late for their appointments and commitments, and not because of an emergency but because of their bad habits. They are absent from commitments because they forget, and then move on as if nothing had happened. They do not even have an agenda for each day or week. No wonder success eludes them, and there is neither promotion, ascension, nor effectiveness. We are experts at improvising, even if it means wasting time, effort, and money. We need to master the science of managing our time. I recommend the book by Newberry already mentioned, especially chapter four.

Many people want to succeed in different areas of their lives, but they do not even know how to organize their time. They steal time from God, family, and studies, but have spare time to talk nonsense with their "fool" of a "friend", and to spend hours sitting in a street corner with a group of mediocre and good-for-nothing people.

Delegate

If you want to maximize your time, you must learn the art of delegation. Your project will require you to learn to delegate, because no one can do everything alone. You need to delegate certain tasks to take care of those other tasks that are really important to you, and need your attention to be completed. This was the advice Jethro gave to Moses in the wilderness (Exodus 18:13-26). He saw him minister to the people from morning until night, resolving all types of disputes, while a group of wise men near him remained inactive as spectators.

Jethro advises Moses to delegate certain tasks to wise men that have his spirit, so he can in turn concern himself with other more important matters. He says if you do this, you will be fine (you will not wear out), and the people will do well (Exodus 18: 13-23). Jethro gives him a crash course in time management. You can maximize your time and be more effective if you learn to delegate. Delegation is an art, because you need to know what to delegate and to whom. Unquestionably, we need to delegate tasks in order to make good use of time.

Procrastination

Your project will also require you to be free from the procrastination syndrome. This term may sound strange, yet it is what many do, even if they do not know what it is called. Procrastination means delaying higher-priority tasks for others of lower priority. It is the art of keeping up with yesterday and avoiding today. [5] You need to drop the excuses that prevent you from doing now what you have to do today. Remember that everything has its season and time under heaven. This brings us to the theme of seasons in life.

Seasons

If we want to manage time well, we must understand the concept of seasons. The beloved in Song of Solomon was living out of season. The winter and the rain had passed, spring had arrived, but she continued living as if it was winter (Song of Solomon 2:10-13). We cannot maximize our time, if we are confused about the season in which we live. Part of the success ants have surviving the winter lies in their ability to distinguish between one season (winter) and the other (summer). During the summer, they remember that it is time to store food for the winter, where there is no food available. In that way, they maximize their summer (Prov. 6:6-8). Every good farmer knows and maximizes the principle of Ecclesiastes 3:1, that everything has its season and time. He knows the right time (season) to plant and to harvest. Because of that, he will not make efforts to plant, when it is time to harvest. Psalm 1:3 says that the tree will bear fruit in its season. What time or season are you living now?

Consider the following: what a teenager is able to do may be deemed acceptable, but wrong and even harmful if done by a child. A teenager can start driving lessons, but not a 5-year old child. A young adult may be engaged to marriage and get married, but not a 12-year old child. Perhaps I have the calling to be a teacher, but first I have to invest time in learning. There are people who want to start their own business, when they do not yet know how to reconcile their own checkbook. Seasons, phases, a time, and an hour for each thing ...

Getting ahead or being late can kill our vision and project. Many sin because of their haste. They lack patience and do not know how to wait for their season, and this connects them with failure. Others sin by their sluggishness. Their season passes and they lose "momentum." If everything has its season, then I have to identify the season of each thing. The apostle Peter wrote that all promotion has its season. If we learn to humble ourselves under the mighty hand of God, in time, we will be exalted. It says in 1 Peter 5:6: "Therefore humble yourselves under the mighty hand of God, that He may exalt you in due time." It is the same message of Galatians 6:9: "And let us not grow weary while doing good, for in due season we shall reap if we do not lose heart." You have to attach to your project the seasonal factor, so that even if certain things are "delayed" you do not grow weary and can stay focused for all of the time necessary.

Let me tell you this: **Big projects take time.** If your goal is to go through a crash course on how to use a cell phone, then a week is sufficient. However, if your goal is to become a scientist, a NASA astronaut, a lawyer, or engineer, then you know such goals imply time. How much time are you willing to invest and wait in favor of your project? Do you dare keep a diary for a month to record how you used the 30 days, hour by hour? Are you willing to change the way you use your time so you can complete your project?

Habakkuk

There are people who fail in their project, because after the passage of some considerable amount time without seeing progress, they abandon it. They mistake the delay with failure, when in fact that waiting time was a fundamental part of the success of their project. Remember, God told the prophet to write the vision, and that even if it took time it would be fulfilled.

> "For the vision is yet for the appointed time; it testifies about the end and will not lie. Though it delays, wait for it, since it will certainly come and not be late."
>
> Habakkuk 2:3 (HCSB)

What God is saying to the prophet is not to take the apparent delay in the vision as a failure, but rather to be patient, because the vision is progressing and moving forward. Even if it takes a little time, wait for it. The vision has stages and seasons; it needs time. Because of that God said to the prophet: "Write the vision; make it plain on tablets, so he may run who reads it." (Habakkuk 2:2). Your vision and your project take time. Your vision needs to be written down, read, and decreed each day to keep it alive, even through the passage of time.

Elisha

The prophet Elijah called Elisha to prepare the young man as his successor, but according to historians, that process took more than 15 years. However, Elisha waited his time and for his moment. We can identify two seasons or two mantles. First, Elisha sees Elijah plowing with the yoke of the oxen, and throws the mantle over him to recruit him as an apprentice of the prophet. Finally, after many years, when Elijah was taken up to heaven, he throws the mantle over him a second time to transfer his function as a prophet. Everything has its season and time.

Chronos and Kairos

If you want to maximize your time, you have to know the difference between Chronos and Kairos. These are two words in Greek meaning time. Although both mean time, there is a great difference between them. Kairos literally means opportunity. It refers to the specific and opportune time for action or to make a decision. Chronos refers to chronological time in seconds, minutes, hours, days, months, years, etc. as we know it. If you go to work at 8 a.m., you better function in Chronos and arrive at the right time.

Time from God's perspective is different. It may be the worst time or the greatest crisis of the decade; however, God says that this is your Kairos. This is your chance, it is your moment to decide and act. The Chronos and Kairos times do not always coincide.

Isaiah 43:19

When the people of Israel received this prophetic word, they were in exile in one of the most critical moments in its history. Even so, God says through the prophet Isaiah, that a new time is coming for them. "Look, I am about to do something new; even now it is coming. Do you not see it? Indeed, I will make a way in the wilderness, rivers in the desert" (HCSB). Again, God will do something new with them; he will make a way in the desert and will turn a dry land into a fertile land. A new era was to be initiated, a new opportunity, and they needed to recognize the new season. Considering the times in which the people were living, that word from the prophet did not make sense. So God says: "even now it is coming. Do you not see it?" It was their Kairos time, and they should not lose it. Your Kairos time can be completely different from your Chronos time.

Your dreams, visions, and projects will need good management of your Chronos time, but also the Kairos time. You must learn to identify your Kairos time: Do you not see it? If you are not careful, if you do not know the difference, if you do not identify the new season or you do not take advantage of your Kairos chance, your project will be affected, and you can miss the new things of God. You need to learn to recognize your new season. It is a danger to sustain your project by considering only the Chronos time. Your project requires you to manage your Chronos time as well as your Kairos time. Maximize them! Take advantage of them! And manage them well. The success of your project is linked to the good use of the time factor, because everything has its season and time under heaven.

Notes

1) Tommy Newberry, <u>Success Is Not an Accident: Change Your Choices; Change Your Life</u>, p. 95-96

2) Mike Murdock, <u>The Law of Recognition</u>, pp. 210-212

3) Tommy Newberry, <u>Success Is Not an Accident: Change Your Choices; Change Your Life</u>, p. 94

4) Ibid. p. 98

5) Ibid. p. 104

Guiding Questions - Chapter Two

1) Write the principle established in Eccl. 3:1 and Eph. 5:6.

2) Explain the author's quote: "Good things done out of season run the risk of being unproductive." Give examples.

3) Why is it important to recognize the time factor for the success of your project?

4) What are the five priorities in your life? How much time do you assign to each?

5) Do you consider yourself an organized person that maximizes the use of time? Explain.

6) Why is delegating tasks to others key to the success of your projects?

7) What is procrastination? Have you experienced this symptom in your life? Explain.

8) Explain the concept of seasons shared by the author. What is the importance of this concept for the propelling of your project?

9) Share some biblical examples the author gives to prove his thesis: "Big projects take time."

10) Explain the difference between Chronos and Kairos.

3ᴿᴰ POWERFUL PRINCIPLE: DECISIONS

The principle that impacts your future

Choose whom you will serve ... but as for me
and my house, we will serve the LORD.
Joshua 24:15

Your project will depend on the good decisions you make throughout your life. The progress and success of your projects is closely linked to your decision-making: your ability to answer yes or no to the demands of life. We all need to pay attention to our decision-making process, because during our lifetime we have to make choices. How effective are you when making decisions? How much value do you give to this process? How do you arrive at a decision? Do you imitate others or follow the fads? Do you make decisions just to go against someone else? Do you make decisions based on emotions or impulses? Do you make important decisions quickly and without thinking?

People who have been successful throughout their lives have distinguished themselves by taking seriously their decision-making power. Minimizing and under-valuing the decision-making process has led many businesses into bankruptcy, has caused divorces, illnesses and deaths. "The only true freedom each of us has in life is the freedom to choose. But once we choose, we become the servant of our choices." [1]

The pastor Creflo Dollar says that life is itself a continuous series of decisions, and emphasizes that the challenge goes beyond making decisions, but rather making wise choices and quality decisions. [2]

Let me share with you some thoughts on the importance and power of decision-making. Read, meditate, and analyze them.

- Decisions set the course of your life and your project.
- You are today what you decided yesterday, and will be tomorrow what you decide today.
- The future of your project will be as strong as the decisions that preceded it.
- Every decision you make will have an effect on your quality of life.
- The decisions you choose make you who you are.
- Your decisions will truly show who you are, more than your speech and your skills. There is no need to examine your "curriculum vitae," we only need to observe the decisions you have made.
- The decisions you make not only affect you but your family, your friends, and your projects.
- Decisions are like dominoes, as they fall each will have irreversible consequences on the other.

Esau (Genesis 25:29-34)

Esau lost his birthright because he made a bad decision. He made a major decision in a moment of weariness and hunger. Though later he attempted to recover his birthright, his efforts were in vain. He had to live the rest of his life with the consequence of a poor decision.

You should never make crucial decisions under the influence of strong emotions or under time pressure and in haste. Decisions such as marriage, divorce, property purchases, or a job change made under such conditions can lead you to the Esau syndrome.

Joshua (24:13-17)

Joshua is an interesting case as it pertains to the decision-making process. He stood before all the people and proclaimed that he had made an important decision, and that he would stand firm in his decision independent of their choice. Joshua said:

> "And if it seems evil to you to serve the LORD, choose for yourselves this day whom you will serve, whether the gods which your fathers served that were on the other side of the River, or the gods of the Amorites, in whose land you dwell. **But as for me and my house, we will serve the LORD.**"
>
> Joshua 24:15

Joshua did not make the decision based on people's opinion. The majority is not always correct or in the right. In fact, the apostle Paul tells us not to be conformed to this world, but take care to discern God's will for our lives (Romans 12:2). Joshua was willing to pay the price of a good decision, even if no one else decided like him; he was willing to withstand the social pressure. How willing are you to decide for what is right, even if most people are choosing the opposite? Are you willing to risk negotiating acceptance and comfort even if it means making bad decisions?

The Prodigal Son (Luke15:11-20)

The prodigal son lost his inheritance and went completely bankrupt, of not only money but also food, clothing, shelter, friendship, and family, all because of a bad decision. His entire quality of life was affected by the fatal decision to leave his father's house with his inheritance. It really was not the time to leave his house, nor was it the time to receive his inheritance. Then he did not choose the best place to live or the best of friends; he decided wrongly about how to live (he lived desperately). He later accepted that he had made bad choices, and that what he was experiencing was the result of his bad decision. In that moment, the prodigal son then makes a good decision that again affected his future, this time for his wellbeing. See how the decisions of this young man affected his life for better or for worse. Unquestionably, it is still so today.

As a pastor, I continually encounter the Esau syndrome and the syndrome of the prodigal son, but few are the times when I encounter the Joshuas. Many couples have come to me so I could marry them, despite having only known each other for several months. They do not come to consult, to ask for prayer, to enter into a counseling process to see if their decision to join in marriage is really a good one. Instead, they come with a wedding date; God already spoke to them. They love each other, understand each other perfectly, and everything is hunky-dory.

Let me tell you that 90 percent of those couples that have come to me in that condition have failed in their relationships or if they are still together are in a dysfunctional marriage. They do not separate so that people do not say they were mistaken, which itself is another mistake, because the reason they stay together is negative. Some of these relationships have lasted less than six months after the wedding. It turned out they really did not know each other, and lacked valuable information about each other. Similarly, brethren have come to me with a decision taken lightly about their businesses, partnerships, and relocation; these have had the same results, ending in failure.

How to make the best decisions

Decision-making then is an important process that you should not ignore. How can you make the best decisions throughout your life? Bishop TD Jakes wrote a book on this subject called: **Before You Do: Making Great Decisions That You Won't Regret**. I recommend that you read this book if you want to grow in the area of decision-making. It should be mandatory reading for the youth. Let me share with you some steps that Bishop Jakes lists when making crucial decisions.

Step 1

Making good decisions begins when people recognize the power and importance of decisions. This places them in a position of respect and care when making crucial decisions. In that way, they will have an advantage over those that take the process lightly. Do you recognize and value the importance of decisions?

Step 2

Making good decisions has to do with identity and vocation. People who know who they are (identity) and what they want to do, know what is truly important (vocation), and can decide with more clarity and without future regrets. This implies that one of the first things you should invest time in is to know yourself. You should know what is your potential, your gifts and abilities, your purpose, your calling, and so on. TD Jakes says:

> "[Learn] to make decisions in the moment based on who you truly are, and taking actions based on love, kindness, and forgiveness ..." [3]

That way you will make decisions that are consistent and appropriate with your vision, and instead of holding you back, they will propel you. In fact, I do not have to make the same decisions as everyone else, because my criteria for making decisions are based on my identity and vocation. If I know who I am, then I have criteria by which to decide well. Where do you find yourself concerning your identity and vocation?

I remember well a time when I had to make an important decision, one that was based on my calling and vocation. After graduating from college, I applied for a job as a music teacher in Puerto Rico's Department of Public Education. I needed to find not just any job, but one that was in a nearby town, because in six months I would marry Loyda in addition to having responsibilities as an assistant pastor and the leader of a Christian music group. All of the teaching positions of the nearby towns were full. I was offered two teaching positions, but both required me to move far away from my house, church, and Loyda. I did not want to resign from any of these positions, because I knew my calling and vocation. I also needed to be near Loyda in those months leading up to the wedding. Even though I needed to work, I decided to wait, pray, and believe God.

Before a month of waiting had gone by, the music teacher from the town of Loiza, where the church was located and

Loyda lived, and just minutes from Rio Grande where I lived, decided to resign. They then called me to be the music teacher in the high school of Loiza. The school was three minutes from my mother-in-law's house, where I would go to eat lunch (a good one and free), and where I would later share with my baby girl Idaelis, who was born a year after we wedded, since my mother-in-law took care of her during the day. Above all, I was able to continue as an assistant pastor at the church, and to go out with the music group to different churches during the week. Praise God!

Step 3

Making good decisions requires being informed. This is the step where you investigate. It is the part of the process where you collect valuable and relevant information. People who make good decisions first invest time to research their options. You cannot believe everything they say out there; you have to investigate and go to necessary sources. Consult with the relevant people, both professionals, spiritual leaders, friends or family, to have a clearer picture, a more complete picture, see the pros and cons, and minimize surprises. [4] Do not be afraid to ask questions. "Research fuels your decisions by yielding the information on which you can base a sound decision ... You can never know more than you are willing to ask." [5] Any sound decision is sustained by valuable information.

Step 4

Making good decisions requires the analysis of the data collected to be as objective as possible. That is, to enter into a process of reflection and discernment in light of all of the information received. Some people receive information, but then ignore it. Discernment is a rare virtue that few develop, but it is extremely important when making decisions. Remember that not everything that glitters is gold. "Good decision making in relationships, business, anything, results from a process of reflection-discernment-decision." [6]

We live in a society of lies, appearances, facades, where people take advantage of the naiveté, inexperience, and good hearts of others in order to take advantage or gain some benefit from them. Listen to this: decision-making is not just a matter of heart (emotions), but also of the head (reason). "Both sets of factors - your head and your heart - must come into the equation in making ... any significant decision." [7] This is the principle that Paul teaches in Philippians 1:9-10.

> "And this I pray, that your love may abound still more and more in knowledge and all discernment, that you may approve the things that are excellent..."

To love (feelings) we must add knowledge (information), so we can then make the best decisions; that is to approve the things that are excellent, and not approve anything we might later come to regret. This is the formula that Paul taught the Philippians. Your project demands that you approve those things that are excellent. Do not leave your head out of the process; do not make decisions under emotional or soulish effects. Do not give so much power to your soul. It is not that you leave out your emotions, but rather that you do not neglect reason.

Step 5

Making good decisions requires time and effort. People who make good decisions are well aware of this. Time is needed to gather information, analyze and discern, and pray to God for wisdom and direction. All of that also requires effort.

Your project is so important that it is worth investing time and effort, especially if you want to avoid problems and headaches later. Nowadays people want everything fast and easy. Few are willing to invest time and energy. I repeat: crucial decisions take time and effort. Do not let pressure take you to a place where you abort this process. Pay the price.

Procrastination

The problem for many people is the fear of deciding. In the previous chapter, we talked about this syndrome. These are the ones who decide not to decide. Even with information and knowing what really suits them, they are afraid to decide, and postpone the decision from one day to the next. They are afraid to fail, to make mistakes, or to be judged by people. This is just as dangerous as a bad decision. Your project requires you to make good decisions at the right time, because opportunities have expiration dates, open doors that at a certain point will close. Many have delayed their project, because they failed to make good and timely decisions.

As the wise village elder would say: "Never put off for tomorrow what you can do today." Do not postpone the time to make decisions. Research, discern, pray, and then decide. If you are mistaken in something, you have in your favor that you did your part; you followed a good decision-making process. It is time to improve your process for making good decisions. You will be tomorrow what you decide today.

If you do not like what you are living now, then begin to make better decisions today to positively affect your tomorrow.

Notes

1) John Maxwell, <u>The Choice is Yours,</u> Introduction, p. 6
2) Creflo Dollar, <u>8 Steps to Create the Life You Want: The Anatomy of a Successful Life</u>, pp. 4-5
3) TD Jakes, <u>Before You Do: Making Great Decisions That You Won't Regret</u>, p. 7
4) Ibid, p. 29
5) Ibid, p. 26-27
6) Ibid, p. 15
7) Ibid, p. 18

Guiding Questions - Chapter Three

1) Explain John Maxwell's quote that says that the only true freedom we have is to choose, and that once a decision is made we are servants to it.
2) The author shares eight statements about the importance and value of decision making to the success of your project. Choose three and explain them.
3) What lessons are we taught by Esau, the prodigal son, and Joshua about decision-making?
4) What is the first step to making good decisions?
5) Why does being clear about who we are and where we are going help us to make smarter decisions?
6) Explain and give your opinion on what Bishop TD Jakes says: "Research fuels your decisions by yielding the information on which you can base a sound decision."

7) Whom are you accustomed to consulting when it comes time to make decisions?

8) What is the danger of making decisions in haste, under strong emotions, and without the necessary information?

9) The author says that today's society has become accustomed to having everything fast and easy. How can this condition affect the decision making process?

10) Explain the phrase: "We are today what we decided yesterday, and will be tomorrow what we decide today."

4TH POWERFUL PRINCIPLE: MONEY

*The principle that increases your options
and your influence*

A feast is made for laughter, and wine makes
merry; but money answers everything.
Ecclesiastes 10:19

Your project will need money. Your vision will need to be funded. Even if you assume a highly spiritual position, your plans will still need money. Some get overly spiritual when this subject is broached, and say, "all I need is God." I understand the perspective of those who think this way, but their position reveals a limited understanding about money. Nehemiah was a man of God, a spiritual man given to prayer and fasting, who decided to complete the vision God gave him. When the king asks him what he needs, he does not say, "no thanks, I have God." Let us look at his reply. In chapter 2:5-9, he asks the king for:

- Permission to leave the palace and go rebuild the city
- Letters to the governors of the provinces, allowing him free pass through their territories
- Wood to repair the city gates, the walls, and their homes

Like Nehemiah's project, your project will need material provision. You need to relate properly with the financial aspects of your project, for your understanding and management of the money that reaches your hands will either propel or delay your project. I sincerely believe that God's children urgently need to do two things concerning money, namely:

1) Review our thinking or understanding of money
2) Acquire knowledge, skills, and tools that allow us to manage money in an excellent and productive way

Review our mindset concerning money

We need to revisit our understanding of money, because many have been operating on myths, fears, lies, and half-truths. The truth is that money increases your chances, choices, and your power to influence. Having greater choices and influence will help the progress of your project. That was the declaration of the preacher in Ecclesiastes 10:19b **"money answers everything."** The reality is you will always find ways in which to use, spend, or invest money.

Christians have been operating in a spirit of confusion and contradiction. On the one hand, many pastors teach their congregations that money is evil, that riches spoil us, that being poor is a virtue, and that we ought to renounce financial abundance. On the other hand, they require them to bring money (tithes and offerings) to church in order to be able to assume the costs of the ministry and the plans to buy new vehicles, land, buildings, and radio stations, among other things. What contradiction is this?

Some time ago, I heard that kind of exhortation through a radio station. The broadcaster preached and criticized the so-called "prosperity preachers," but a week later they were conducting a fundraiser marathon. They suspended all programming for several days to ask for money, in order to be able pay and support the radio station. They have God, but they need money. At the same time, they were announcing a bazaar, where they were to sell items and clothing at low prices to raise money for the ministry. First point: Their project needed money, but the critical part was that they were asking the same people who they were teaching not have any money. What contradiction is this? What is your understanding of money?

Many pastors are praying for a businessman to enter through the doors of their church with a million dollar check. However, they do not dare to visualize that businessman or businesswoman as a member of their church. Why is it acceptable for a millionaire from outside the congregation to bless me, instead of a millionaire from inside the church?

Friends and brethren, money is amoral. Its good or evil depends on how you use it. You can buy drugs that damage your body or buy medicine and food to send to developing countries like Somalia. Having large amounts of money does not necessarily harm a person. Do not confuse the text of 1 Timothy 6:10. It is not money that is the root of all evil, but rather the love of money. The danger is when we put money above God, and we stop trusting in Him.

What is your concept about money? Is it negative or suspicious? Your answer will have much to do with the advancement or delay of your project. The Word gives us certain warnings about the use of money that are worth knowing and not overlooking. For example, the Word warns against greed, idolatry, materialism, and the love of money. These warnings are valid, and anyone seeking to manage money better not underestimate them because many people have fallen because of money (see 1 Tim. 6:9-10).

The advice of 1 Timothy 6:9-10 in no way captures all that the scriptures teach about money and finances. There are many of other texts and scriptures that also give valuable information. Let us consider some of these passages. In Haggai 2:8 God says, "The silver is Mine, and the gold is Mine." Deuteronomy 8:18 tells us: "And you shall remember the LORD your God, for it is He who gives you power to get wealth." 1 Chronicles 29:12 declares that not only the glory proceeds from God, but also the riches.

> "Both riches and honor come from You, and You reign over all. In Your hand is power and might; In Your hand it is to make great and to give strength to all."

If God is the master of riches, and He wants to give their children the power to get wealth, what is the problem?

Consider the glory of God. In every meeting, we ask for the glory of God and talk about it. The traditional church has no problem with the glory of God, though they have problems with the riches. Let me tell you this: where the glory of God is found, there will be wealth. **Glory and wealth are connected.** This is the truth found in Philippians 4:19, Isaiah 60:1, 5 and 11, and Haggai 2:7-9. The house of Obed-edom and his descendants prospered in all things and all he had was blessed. The reason for his blessing was that the Ark of the Covenant, which represents the glory and the holy presence of God, was in his home for three months.

You need to readjust your concept of wealth and money. Again, money provides power and influence, and expands our options for action.

Peter Wagner says in his book **Dominion!: How Kingdom Action Can Change the World** that sociologists have identified three factors that have power and influence in the transformation of cities, namely: violence, knowledge and money. [1] That agrees with the preacher of Ecclesiastes, who says that money answers everything (Ecclesiastes 10:19b). When I lack money, I stand in a limited position. If your project has no money, it is at a disadvantage. Operating with debt, deficit, or in bankruptcy is not the same as operating with provision and surplus.

When we go to different banks to seek funding for our projects, bank managers are amazed by the manner in which we administer the finances of our church. Seeing our financial reports audited for the past eight years by a professional accounting firm gives them confidence to do business with us. Good money management attracts attention, better treatment, and more options.

The way you manage your money opens or closes doors. Do you know your credit score? Do you know your credit history? Those with better credit scores will receive the best financial offers; that is to have an advantage and greater choices. The banker is not interested in seeing your college degree or your academic achievements. He wants to know the credit score and reports provided by the three major credit bureaus. The banker is not in the business of lending money to people who do not pay or do not have financial security. It is time you give this area the importance it deserves. Valuing these financial aspects reflects on your vision and your management of money. Your credit score can be improved, but it will not happen automatically. Your project needs your credit score to improve every day.

We have to destroy the myths and half-truths that the spirit of religiosity has infiltrated through the church. These have brought fear and a false understanding of piety that is linked with poverty and the lack of money. We are often presented with examples of people who were corrupted by money or fell from grace because of money. It is true that there are and there will be such examples. However, the Bible has many models of men and women of God who were spiritual, effective, and at the same time rich, or said differently, not poor. What happens is that tradition has chosen to promote some characteristics of their profiles over others.

Consider Abraham. In his traditional profile, he is known as the father of faith, a friend of God, and an intercessor; but the Bible also says that he was very rich in cattle, silver, and gold (Gen. 13:1-2). The same goes for Isaac (Gen. 26:13), Jacob, Jabez, David, Job, Daniel and his three friends, and so on. Also, consider Ruth when she marries Boaz, Lydia of Thyatira, Cornelius, and Joseph of Arimathea among others. All were rich and spiritual, used by God, but this aspect of their financial status tends to be overlooked.

If you understand that you need money and funding for your project, but also pray rebuking all prosperity, money, multiplication, growth, transfer of wealth, power to get wealth, gold and silver, then you live in a contradiction that voids and impoverishes your project. You urgently need to renew your understanding about money and about the prosperity of the kingdom.

Acquire knowledge: administrative tools

Despite having to continually manage money, the people of God live in great ignorance about how to manage finances well. Many of us are like a five-year old who does not know the difference between a one-dollar bill and a one hundred dollar bill. If you give him a choice, the child will make a random decision not based on knowledge. Many of us act in this way as it pertains to money.

You are unaware of important information about how to maximize money, so that you can move forward from having to work for money to having money working for you. You need to have more knowledge, skills, and tools to be good money manager. Money is not just for spending; it is also for investing and multiplying it. That is why God gives seed to the sower and bread to the one who eats (2 Cor. 9:10). You need to develop a sower and investor mentality so that you do not eat the seeds along with the bread. Your project needs your good financial management.

One of the objectives of the Shalom seminar [2] is to help participants develop a financial budget and abide by it. It also teaches people to pay off debt, to avoid new debt, to save and invest, and multiply their money. Most people do not know exactly how much they earn, how much they spend, nor what they spend it on. That is alarming. The vast majority live in debt, paying high interest, not having developed the habit of saving, are not ready for emergencies or for retirement, and know even less about how to invest their money. They are experts in spending, but not in saving or multiplying their money. Can your project prosper under those conditions?

A lesson from the Jews

Jews stand out because, in addition to the knowledge they are expected to get through the school system and the Torah (the principles of their faith), they teach their children and youth the value of money. They teach them how to conduct business and how to increase money. They teach them how the stock market and Wall Street works. They do not wait until their children are adults, rather they train them as children, and not just those who are going into business, but instead they teach everyone. In the Jewish faith, there is no contradiction whatsoever between being faithful to God and being prosperous in all areas, including their finances. We Christians have that conflict. Young Jews grow with a mentality of progress and with the information and skills necessary to be good stewards and for good money management. [3] For more information on this subject, I recommend the book by Pastor John Muratori, **Rich Church, Poor Church**.

Many of us are more like the wicked and lazy servant, than the other two servants presented in the parable of Matthew 25:14-39. The lazy servant who was given a "hundred dollars" did not know how to handle money, or how to multiply it. For that reason he hid the money in a hole in the ground. It is true that he did not lose money, but neither did he increase it. The two reasons for his failure were fear and ignorance. He did not even know that there were banks that could earn him interest on the money. This was part of the reproof given to him by the Lord. The Lord expected all three servants to multiply the money. This involved understanding and good management.

I urge you to prepare and equip yourself in the area of money management. Attend courses and seminars regarding money management. Buy and read books on this subject, and get a mentor to help you grow in this area. Please organize your finances and maximize your money. If your finances look a lot like a plate of spaghetti, then it will be difficult for your project to develop and progress.

Your project requires a renewal of your mindset about finances, driving out all the myths, fears, and half-truths. It also requires you to have financial freedom, good sources of information, and an excellent handling of money. It is never too late to learn. Set as a goal to be a person that is not only free of debt but has financial freedom. Your project needs funding.

Notes

1) Peter Wagner, <u>Dominion!: How Kingdom Action Can Change the World,</u> p. 181

2) The Shalom seminar is a series of theological and practical conferences prepared by Apostle Osorio, seeking to help God's children, as well as churches, achieve financial freedom in order to advance the agenda of the Kingdom.

3) John Muratori, <u>Rich Church Poor Church: Unlock the Secrets of Creating Wealth and Harness the Power of Money to Influence Everything</u>, p. 93-103

Guiding Questions - Chapter Four

1) Do you agree with the author when he says that your project will need money, and that accepting this reality does not make you less spiritual? Share the example of Nehemiah and the king.

2) According to the author, what are the two most important areas we must resolve about money in order to propel our project?

3) What two things does the money do in our favor?

4) What is your concept of money? Explain the phrase: Money is amoral.

5) Write down some of the biblical warnings about the use of money appearing in 1 Tim. 6:9-10. Comment on it.

6) Name some passages from the Scriptures that offer us the other side of the coin (the positive part) concerning money. Can you find others?

7) Explain some of the myths and half-truths about money.

8) Explain the statement: "The way you manage your money opens or closes doors." Do you consider yourself a good money manager?

9) Why is it important to develop a sower and investor mentality? Explain the parable of the talents in light of the teaching of this chapter (Matthew 25:14-39).

10) What things can you do to improve your ability to manage more effectively your money and finances?

5th Powerful Principle: Faith

The principle that conquers the impossible

The just shall live by faith
Hebrews 10:38

Making your project a reality requires you to be a person of faith. The first person that has to believe in your project and your vision is you. Without faith, your project is in danger of dying. **People of faith have an advantage over those who operate in a spirit of doubt and disbelief.**

To make your project a reality, you need many things to be released through faith. Faith in God is not optional or a luxury, it is an indispensable prerequisite. Jesus taught this to his disciples and said to them: "Have faith in God" (Mark 11:22). The writer of the Letter to the Hebrews taught that without faith it is impossible to please God. If we are to establish a relationship with God, we must approach Him in faith. The Word says, "must"; therefore, it is a requirement.

"But without faith it is impossible to please Him, for he who comes to God **must** believe that He is, and that He is a rewarder of those who diligently seek Him."

Hebrews 11:6

Faith is defined in Hebrews 11:1, as the substance of things hoped for, the evidence of things not seen. It is an advantage to see in advance what is not or has not yet been manifested in the natural and the visible. Your project needs you to be able to see what is not yet seen by the natural eye.

Other definitions of faith according to the writer Mike Murdock include:

- Faith is that invisible confidence that something exists other than what you presently see.
- Faith is the magnet that attracts God toward you.
- Faith can transform you from a weakling into the champion God intended you to be.
- Faith is what turns common people into uncommon achievers.
- Faith is a seed planted into the soil of your spirit. [1]

Why do people of faith, who have projects to complete and see realized, have an advantage over those without it?

First, people who have faith have an advantage over those who doubt, because as they operate in faith, they are moving from the natural to the supernatural dimension. In the supernatural dimension, nothing is impossible; there are no limits. On the other hand, in the natural dimension you can only operate at the level of the visible, possible, understandable, logical, and in line with the statistics or probabilities.

When you move in faith, you start to see the invisible in order to bring it forward to the visible; you begin to breakthrough the impossible to bring it to the possible, and start calling things that are not as though they were. Jesus established what I am sharing when He said in Mark 9:23: "all things are possible to him who believes." He who believes increases his advantage over the incredulous, because their faith conquers the impossible, while the others will remain operating only in what is possible. From which dimension are you operating your project?

Secondly, people of faith have an advantage over those who do not activate their faith because they will know how to speak to the mountains of opposition, and relocate them. By now you probably know that large projects experience great obstacles and opposition. You will confront people close and far from you, as well as institutions that will oppose your project. It is here where the mountain movers have an advantage over the rest.

While others are stranded at the foot of the mountain (opposition, limitation, stagnation), people of faith give orders to the mountains to relocate, so they can move forward. Jesus taught his disciples to give orders to the mountains.

> "For assuredly, I say to you, whoever says to this mountain, 'Be removed and be cast into the sea,' and does not doubt in his heart, but believes that those things he says will be done, he will have whatever he says."
>
> Mark 11:23

David, a man of faith, spoke to his giant, and moved him, while King Saul remained full of fear, inert, and passive in the face of the same giant. I do not know what mountains you may be facing now, but it is time to activate your faith and relocate them.

Thirdly, people of faith have an advantage over those who do not believe, because through their faith they will know how to face and manage difficult times. Anyone can have success during times of abundance, but it is during difficult times where people are tested. You must know there will be rather difficult seasons over the length of your project. You will face circumstances outside of your control such as economic recessions or depressions, climate changes, diseases, prejudice, strikes, etc. However, where many give up and surrender, faith will allow you to keep working, because it can stand to the crisis.

Faith will not inoculate you from experiencing seasons of "drought." On the contrary, faith enables and empowers you to manage the crisis. You have to understand the nature of faith. It is in the midst of a crisis, in the difficult time, that faith is activated. Faith is to the crisis as medicine is to pain, shelter to the cold and food to the hungry.

Faith will not prevent you from facing "lions, fire, sword, weakness and armies," but Hebrews 11:33 declares that by faith you can stop the mouths of lions, quench the violence of fire, escape the edge of the sword, draw strength from weakness and turn to flight the armies of the enemies. This is a great advantage, because you already know what you can do through faith when the lions, sword, fire, and enemy armies arrive. Let the lions who want to eat your project beware! For by faith, you will close their mouths.

Hebrews 10:38 says that in the midst of the crisis there are people who will draw back, but others will go forward. The difference lies in that some will live by faith, and not based on the external conditions they face.

"Now the just shall live by faith; but if anyone draws back, My soul has no pleasure in him."

In this verse, the word "live" has a powerful meaning, very different from existing or surviving. Survival's only goal is to make it through another day alive. This implies the possibility of negotiating dreams and goals with their enemies in order to stay alive. It may also include the possibility of stopping or retroceding. On the other hand, living implies energy, courage, strength, enthusiasm, vitality, motivation, and achievement; it is the determination to move forward and fulfill our dreams, goals, and purposes, despite what is happening. This is a great advantage because it connects you with the completion of your project. Are you one of those who have been content surviving or are you living and conquering?

Fourthly, people of faith have an advantage over the doubters, because they will provoke an answer to their prayers. The goal of prayer or the purpose for the one who prays is that their petition be answered. Unfortunately, no matter how much you pray for your project, if your prayer lacks faith, it will fall short. Let me say it this way: Faith is the oxygen of prayer. Without faith, prayer loses its effect; rather, prayer is suffocated. God expects us to ask, but prayer without faith produces nothing.

Jesus taught in Mark 11:24 that faith is what stands between prayer and the result; the connection between prayer and the result is faith.

"Therefore I say to you, whatever things you ask when you pray, believe that you receive them, and you will have them."

James affirms in chapter 5 the key principle of the prayer, that "prayer avails much"; but look at what he says in chapter 1:

"But let him ask in faith, with no doubting, for he who doubts is like a wave of the sea driven and tossed by the wind. For let not that man suppose that he will receive anything from the Lord."

James 1:6-7

Prayer has great power if accompanied by faith; doubt kills prayer. As a pastor I have observed that the reason why some people pray a lot is not because they are steadfast in prayer, but because they do not believe their prayers are being heard; it is not perseverance, but doubt. They stay at the level of pray, pray, pray, but do not go to the next level of believe, believe, believe, in order to receive.

Chapter 11 of the Letter to the Hebrews shares the great results that people like Abel, Enoch, Noah, Abraham, Sarah, Moses, Gideon, David, and others had. What did they all have in common? The principle of faith. Note that each text begins with the phrase "by faith." By faith Abraham... by faith Moses... by faith Gideon... Perhaps each of them was missing many things in their critical moment, but something they all had in common was faith. Faith was an advantage in their favor. Therefore, if Moses and David relied on faith to accomplish their goals, how much more should you and I? Are you a person of faith or are you oscillating between belief and doubt?

Three dimensions of faith

Faith has three dimensions or key expressions that work together. Faith has to affect your eyes (new perspective on what you are viewing), your mouth (a new language to call things as if they already were), and your feet (move you to action).

New Perspective - eyes

By faith you can see what is not yet visible, to bring it to reality. Abraham first saw all his children, by faith, when he dared to look at the sky, and counted the stars as his children (Gen. 15:5-6). Faith wants to touch your eyes. Can you see your project done, completed, and operational even before it becomes a reality in the physical world?

New language - mouth

By faith, we can call those things that do not exist as though they did, in order to bring them to reality (Rom. 4:17). Faith wants to touch your tongue. God changed Abraham and Sarah's name before they became parents of many nations. Therefore, whenever Sarah called her husband "father of multitudes," she was moving in faith, and bringing the impossible to the possible. (Gen. 17:5, 15-16). The woman suffering from bleeding declared her healing before receiving it (Mr. 5: 28). Joel 3:10 says, "Let the weak say, 'I am strong.'" Remember that there is power in your mouth. Words are seeds that will bear fruit (Prov. 18:20-21). Dare to call things that are not as though they were. Can you call the things missing in your project as if they already were?

New walk - Steps of Faith - feet

By faith, you can take concrete steps and move to action. Faith will touch your feet. By faith, Abraham went out to claim the land that would be given him, without knowing where he was going (Gen. 12:1-4, Gen. 13:17). By faith Moses marched with the people across the Red Sea (Heb. 11:29). Isaac dared to sow, opened furrows and watered the seed in a dry and barren land amid a major drought, and by faith he possessed his harvest (Gen. 26:12). Faith is not only contemplation and words, but also action. Activate your feet!

A personal testimony

When I began pastoring in Springfield, Massachusetts, after a year of renting the temple we used for our meetings, we had to move out unexpectedly. We were left with no place to meet at a time when the congregation had grown from 20 to 100 people. A friend pastor temporarily allowed us to meet in their sanctuary, only on Sunday afternoons. During the week, we had to meet in different homes. Nearing completion of the first month, I went into crisis (the soil of faith) because I knew where we were was only temporary.

I knew very little of the city, and did not have contacts. One Saturday morning I went to the basement of my house alone to pray and fast. I was in a crisis: really worried and feeling impotent. I started reading the passage of Abraham and the sacrifice of his son on Mount Moriah (Gen. 22:1-14). I noticed that when God sent the lamb to be sacrificed instead of his son, Abraham called that place Yahweh Yireh, the Lord will provide. So I held on to that word as a rhema word for me, and declared, "filled with faith," Yahweh Yireh, the Lord will also provide the temple where we will meet. After that, I began to rejoice and declare it. The Lord interrupted me and said to my spirit: Do you truly believe that I can provide the place? I said: "Yes, I believe it."

Then he told me: I want you to share it with the church and testify that you already have the place. I protested: "but we do not have the place yet." Then the Lord took me back to the passage, and showed me that Abraham declared twice that God was Yahweh Yireh. The first time was at the foot of the mountain when his son asked for the lamb for the sacrifice. Abraham then said: Yahweh Yireh, before the provision was visible.

The next day (Sunday), as I ended the preaching, with fear and trembling, but in faith and obedience, I told the church that next Sunday we would gather at a new place that we already had. The whole church stood, clapped and shouted. I was dying on the altar, hoping nobody would ask me where it was or how it was, because I did not know. I just told them that during the week each family would be called to be given the address.

That Monday I went around the city in my car (steps of faith), and the Lord stopped me in front of a Methodist Church on Liberty Street. I entered and talked to the pastor and said I was looking to rent a temple for our church. Although we were paying $300 a month in the previous place, I offered him $800 during the winter season and $700 in the other months. I asked to be able to meet on Sundays, Wednesdays, and two Fridays a month. The pastor's response was positive, and he invited me to a meeting with the governing leaders of his church the following evening. I attended the meeting with the treasurer and we received the affirmative call of approval on Thursday.

On Sunday of that week, we had the first service at that sanctuary, which happened to be Thanksgiving Day, and we celebrated with joy, testimonies, and a great dinner. I had to see, speak, and take steps of faith to receive what we needed.

Remember: when you walk in faith, you have an advantage over those who only operate in doubt, unbelief, fears, and worry. Your project needs your faith. Faith will conquer the impossible. The righteous shall live by faith, and so will your project.

Notes

1) Mike Murdock, <u>The Uncommon Dream</u>, p. 85-86

Guide Questions - Chapter Five

1) Write down the principle found in Hebrews 10:30-31 and Hebrews 11:6. Explain.

2) What are some of the definitions of "faith" the author presents?

3) What does the author say regarding people who live and operate in faith over those who constantly live in doubt and fear?

4) Name the four main reasons that cause people of faith to have an advantage over those who doubt.

5) Despite being smaller than Goliath, and not having the military armor, what advantageous element did David possess over the giant that led to his victory? Relate this to Mark 11:23.

6) What mountains have you faced this year relating to your project? How have you faced them?

7) Explain: "Faith pairs up with the crisis, it does not necessarily prevent the crisis, but enables you to face and overcome it."

8) According to the author, what are the three dimensions of faith?

9) Find three Biblical texts for each dimension and explain.

10) How did the author's testimony help you with the difficulties and challenges may be going through regarding your project?

6ᵀᴴ POWERFUL PRINCIPLE: CONFESSION

*The principle that unleashes the power
of life or death*

Death and life are in the power of the tongue,
and those who love it will eat its fruit.
Proverbs 18:21

Your project will also depend on your daily confession, because your confession is powerful. The success, advancement, and progress in any area of your life, is linked to your mouth. To be clear, words are not gone with the wind; rather, the words you confess have an effect over your, your family, and your projects. This is because words are like seeds, as they are released (planted) and time passes, they will bear their fruit. In the same way that seeds are filled with power, so are words. Proverbs 18:21 says: "Death and life are in the power of the tongue..." Then, there is power in words. Each time we speak, we can release death or life, delay or advancement, curse or blessings. What are you releasing each time you speak? What are you confessing about your project?

The proverbialist says that words can be like the piercing of a sword, hurting and even killing (Prov.12: 18). With our words we can hurt, damage or make people sick. The proverbialist also says that words can be like a well of life (Prov. 10:11).

Your words have the power and ability to heal, help, inspire, encourage, and bless others. Jesus cursed the fig tree, and there was one result: it dried up (Mark 11:12-14, 20). On the other hand, Jesus blessed the bread and fish, and they were multiplied to feed a large crowd (Matthew 14:19-20). The results were different, but both were produced by the power of the word. You choose.

Robert Morris, in his book **The Power of Your Words**, says:

- "Words have the capacity to build bridges, span chasms and shorten long distances between you and others." Words can also create distances, barriers and disconnect us from other people.
- "Your words are either building bridges or blowing them up. It's one or the other, because words, more than anything else, connect us to God and to each other." Words not only connect us with other people, but with God through your worship and your prayer.
- "You can determine your future quality of life by the words you speak today." [1]

You must understand that what you speak will come back over you. Before your words affect others, they will affect you first.

> "A man's stomach shall be satisfied from the fruit of his mouth; from the produce of his lips he shall be filled. And... it will eat its fruit."
>
> Proverbs 18:20-21

What did you eat today? What you spoke in the morning will make up your lunch menu. No wonder there is so many children of God with spiritual indigestion. Improve your menu! Be careful with what you confess and talk during the day, because what you say is what you get. Jesus, in accord with the proverbialist, also taught in Mark 11:23: "he will have whatever he says." This principle is too powerful to ignore. It is a danger for you to speak idle, empty, and harmful words, because what you say will be done.

What are you confessing every day about you, your family, your church, your ministry, your project, or your city? Are you confessing words of power and life every day? Or are you talking negatively? Do complaints, gossip, criticism, curses, or concerns spring from your mouth? Are phrases like the following flowing from your mouth: it cannot be done, it is impossible, that effort will fail, this is as far as I go, and I will die tomorrow? Beware; your wish may come true! It is possible that your project is languishing because of your wrong confession.

Paul exhorts the Ephesians to take care of their speech.

> "Let no corrupt word proceed out of your mouth, but what is good for necessary edification, that it may impart grace to the hearers."
>
> Ephesians 4:29

Paul knew the impact of words on the speaker and the hearer. He prohibits the Ephesians from releasing any corrupt words; "no corrupt word" means none. You cannot risk speaking badly and cursing yourself not even in moments of tension or where there is a heavy emotional burden. Those words will have their effect. Liberate yourself from the "Popeye the Sailor" syndrome, who when he was in a bad mood would say, "well, blow me down!" (Note the translation of this phrase in the Spanish show was even more injurious as he would say, "let the devil take me"). With the knowledge you now have, you know that saying so is dangerous. Instead, Paul advises the Ephesians that their words edify and bless their hearers. The scriptures teach that we will be justified or condemned by our words, and that we will give account for every idle word before God.

> "But I say to you that for every idle word men may speak, they will give account of it in the day of judgment. For by your words you will be justified, and by your words you will be condemned."

> Matthew 12:36-37

Confession is an active part of faith. Paul tells the Romans that a man believes with the heart, but "with the mouth confession is made" (Rom. 10:8-10). Each tenet of faith needs to be confessed. Faith needs an external expression. It is not enough to believe, it must be confessed. You need to connect heart and mouth, belief and confession. Without that combination, you will be left incomplete. The Word has to be so close to your heart as well as your mouth. From this principle emerges the power of the prophetic word, the anointing and prophetic service. The power of the prophet lies in his mouth.

Words are not only seeds and have power, but they have a prophetic dimension.

The prophet announces the future. Words, in their prophetic dimension, create your future and affect your destiny. Each time you announce failure, illness, and death before the year-end, you are prophesying about yourself. Joshua, Caleb, and the ten spies are a clear example of what I just expressed. The ten spies prophesied that they could not defeat the giants and that their future was to die in the desert and that is what they received. However, Joshua and Caleb prophesied their victory and that they would conquer the land. They prophesied that they could because the Lord was with them, and that is what they received; they were the only two of their generation that entered the Promised Land (Numbers 13:25-33, 14:1-9).

Prophesy the promises of God for you, prophesy the rhema word that you have received, and prophesy that the unique and special plan of God for your life will be fulfilled according to Jeremiah 29:11. Who do you resemble the most: the ten spies or Joshua and Caleb?

Jeremiah did not know the potential and capacity he had in his mouth, and because of that, he told God: "I cannot speak, for I am a youth" (1:6). God has to then say that he had placed His words into his mouth (Jer. 1:9), and that those words were powerful to such a degree that they could tear, destroy, ruin and overthrow, as well as plant and build (1:10). It is sad that you do not know the full potential God has placed in you, because in ignorance you cannot maximize what you have. God's will is for all his children have the power in their mouth to uproot (that which slows them down) and plant (that which they need). Jeremiah was not an isolated case. God does not want his children to be silent, timid, and unable to unleash the power of God through their mouths. It is time to activate the power that God has placed in your life. Your project will have many things that have to be uprooted and removed that are not allowing it to thrive. By this, I mean environments, curses, plots of the enemy, and even people who have infiltrated your project. Do not say you do not know how to speak. Receive the anointing of Jeremiah.

When you choose to stay quiet, mute, or silent, instead of releasing a powerful word, you put yourself in a common position of disadvantage. The enemy is more powerful when you choose to remain silent, because that self-limits your power and authority. It is true that talking bad or talking more than you ought is dangerous, but to remain silent in order to avoid those pitfalls turns into an even greater mistake.

In life, it is just as bad to speak poorly or talk too much, as it is to remain silent.

Do not allow pain, adverse circumstances, criticism, and attacks to silence or muzzle you. Your project needs you to activate the power in your mouth. These adverse circumstances require that you proclaim, claim, declare, decree, and rebuke. Prophesy over your life, your family, and your project. Declare what Psalm 65:5-9, Job 9:10 and Nehemiah 2: 20 says. Declare the Lord's promises and the rhema word that you have received for your life and your project.

After being forgiven and in his path to restoration, one of the first things David asked God was open his lips again and reactivate his mouth.

> "O Lord, open my lips, And my mouth shall show forth Your praise."
>
> Psalm 51:15

Sin had silenced the prophetic psalmist's mouth, but he could bear it no more. He refused to remain silent for the rest of his life. He said in Psalm 30:11-12:

> "You have turned for me my mourning into dancing; You have put off my sackcloth and clothed me with gladness, To the end that my glory may sing praise to You and not be silent. O LORD my God, I will give thanks to You forever."

What good is a silent sentinel? What good is a silent prophet, preacher, psalmist, worshiper, or intercessor? The effectiveness of these ministries is connected to the mouth.

Look at what Mike Murdock says in his book, **The Uncommon Dream**, about the power of confession and your projects:

- Your conversations need to amplify your dream.
- God has given you a mouth and a mind to magnify your strength, to increase your capability.
- Your words reveal whether you are wise or a fool. [2]

Words are powerful because they create and transform environments.

The success of many of the things that you undertake will depend also on the environment where they are realized. An environment is the spiritual atmosphere that moves or rules, and that affects everything that happens in that place. Many times, I go to places where I want to leave immediately, because they are suffocating environments. They are environments that are negative, with contention, moodiness, depression, gossip, illness, and death. They are literally thrones where demons rest. Many companies have gone bankrupt because customers were scared off by those environments. Many of these environments are caused by the language and attitudes of those who interact there every day. On the other hand, what a difference when you get to a place that breathes peace and life! One wants to stay there. This type of environment refreshes and invigorates you.

I repeat: words and positive confession have the ability to transform heavy-laden environments into environments of Shalom, of Peace. The proverbialist said, "a soft answer turns away wrath" (Prov. 15:1). A soft answer has the effect of changing the environment: it turns away wrath. Psalm 22:3 says that God inhabits the praises of his people. The praise (positive language) is preparing a special throne for God to dwell, and I assure you that such an environment will be different. In an atmosphere of praise miracles, wonders and healings occur, and there will be joy.

Paul and Silas, throughout the night, changed the atmosphere of the prison cell in Philippi. An atmosphere of gloom, grief, pessimism and death, became a place of glory and power. Instead of a prison and entrapment, deliverance was released; instead of death, there was life and salvation. The prison became a temple where the jailer, on his knees, accepted the Lord (see Acts 16:25-32).

It is time to transform the environment of your project. Set free life, power, excitement, blessing, encouragement, joy, success, and victory with your words. Say as the Psalmist: "This is the day the LORD has made; we will rejoice and be glad in it." (Psalm 118:24). "Stop speaking death over your health, your finances, your marriage and your other relationships. Start allowing your mouth to line up with the Word of God." [3] Your project needs your positive confession. Do not stay silent, do not confess evil; unleash the power of life for your project. Activate the prophetic anointing in your mouth, now!

Notes

1) Robert Morris, The Power of Your Words: How God Can Bless Your Life Through the Words You Speak, pp. 20, 30-31

2) Mike Murdock, The Uncommon Dream, pp. 107, 110

3) Robert Morris, <u>The Power of Your Words: How God Can Bless Your Life Through the Words You Speak,</u> p. 31

Guiding Questions - Chapter Six

1) Write the principle of confession found in Prov. 18:21. Explain.

2) Explain whether it is true or not that words are gone with the wind.

3) Give some bible verses showing the power of the word in operation, unleashing both life and death. How does this affect you?

4) Discuss your thoughts on the Robert Morris' opinion on the power of words.

5) What are you confessing every day about yourself, your family, your finances and your project?

6) Explain Matthew 12:36-37.

7) Explain the connection between heart and mouth, belief and faith, and their importance according to Romans 10:8-10.

8) Explain why the words are like seeds, and explain the prophetic dimension of words.

9) The author writes in life it is just as bad to speak poorly or talk too much, as it is to remain silent. Explain. Use the example of David.

10) How do words create and transform environments? Give examples. Why are environments important in relation to your project?

7ᵗʰ Powerful Principle: Perseverance

The principle that refuses to surrender

And let us not grow weary while doing
good, for in due season we shall reap if we
do not lose heart.
Galatians 6:9

I can assure you, without a doubt, that it is not possible to succeed and be effective propelling your project without persistence being part of your profile. You may be a person filled with talent, education, intelligence, and money, but without persistence, you will not get anywhere.

The dictionary defines the words **persist** and **persevere** as continuing in a course of action. To continue speaks of duration. Until when? Until you get what you want, that which you started. This is important because many have the weakness of starting many projects or visions, but completing very few of them. **If you want success, you have to know and walk in the principle of persistence.**

The prophet Oscar Diaz defines persistence in his book, **The law of persistence,** as:

- A principle of power and breakthrough that enables you to face oppositions and struggles, both in the natural and spiritual realm.
- The power of God that keeps you active, dynamic, enterprising, and helps you walk with expectation.
- The key that allows you to fulfill your destiny and achieve your goals. [1]

For Dr. Myles Munroe, persistence is:

- The product of faith that is generated by a purpose.
- The power to hold on, in spite of everything.
- The power to endure.
- The ability to face defeat again and again and not give up.
- The knack for pushing on in the face of difficulty, knowing that victory is yours. [2]

John Maxwell adds:

- Great works are performed not by strength but by perseverance (quoting Charles Johnson).
- If you want success in life, make perseverance your bosom friend (quoting Joseph Addison).
- Before perseverance, "difficulties disappear and obstacles vanish into air" (quoting John Quincy Adams). [3]

To William Feather success is largely a matter of hanging on where others have let go. For Napoleon Hill, effort only fully releases its reward after a person refuses to quit. To Conrad Hilton, successful people keep moving, and although they make mistakes, they do not quit. For Anne Frank, all great achievements require time, patience, and perseverance. [4]

Where does persistence come from?   From where is it nourished?

People tend to be persistent when they have a firm understanding of their purpose, know where they are going, and are confident that they will arrive there. Your persistence is the manifestation of the conviction you have about your future, based on the visions you have been given for your life. The vision affects you; it marks you and allows you to see the future. The conviction of knowing that this vision will take place feeds your persistence. Dr. Munroe said: "True leaders believe that the attainment of their purposes is not optional, but that it is an obligation and a necessity, so they would never think of giving up." [5]

Why do you need to be persistent?

First, because dreams, visions, projects and ministries you have been charged with demand and require a large investment of time. Great visions take time. Great things are not built in a day, and sometimes take generations. Therefore, if you want to progress in achieving your visions or goals, you need persistence and patience. Even if you spend days, weeks and years, you can keep yourself actively engaged in completing your project.

Take the case of Joshua in the conquest of Jericho. The element of persistence was key to achieving his goal. For six days, Joshua summoned the people in the morning, organized them in a specific way, under a strict protocol, marched around the walled city, and then returned to their camp. On the seventh day, they circled the city seven times following the same order and protocol. Only at the end of the seventh round, could they shout and blow the trumpets, and then see the result of persistence (and see how the walls were falling). Seven long days and 13 long laps around the entirety of that great wall.

Today we have many people with great enthusiasm and commitment, but only for two or three laps. When they see that "nothing is happening," they refuse to give it one more lap. When they see that things do not happen in the time they want, they get discouraged and give up. However, Joshua-style leaders know that their goals require time, effort, and consistency. That is why they snatch the victory and achieve the realization of their dreams – because of their persistence. They give all they have to "going around the wall," and they invest whatever time is necessary.

Second, we need persistence, because our projects and goals will experience opposition of all kinds. Persistent people know that the way towards the realization of their goals is not a clear path, wide, bright, safe, and surrounded only by people who encourage and help you. It is a journey with many obstacles and oppositions. You will find opposition in other people who understand that their assignment is to prevent you reaching your goals. This includes spiritual opposition and comprises the kingdom of darkness Ephesians 6:11-12 speaks of. The worst of cases is when there is an alliance between the human and spiritual dimension to stop your ministry, your purpose and project.

This was the case with:

- Joseph, who was sold into slavery and had to unjustly spend time in jail.
- Daniel with the other government leaders who were jealous of him and conspired against him.
- Nehemiah who was opposed in his mission by Sanballat, Tobiah, and Geshem the Arab.

- Paul, who received opposition from Gentiles, Jews, and even his own brethren in the faith.

Pressure comes everyday through criticism, ridicule, accusations, slander, conspiracy and persecution; attacking your reputation with the sole purpose of making you give up and throw in the towel. Therefore, your project needs you to be persistent in order to overcome all types of opposition and obstacles. Nehemiah was a persistent leader. He refused to resign, despite all of Sanballat's strategies. He told the opposition: "The God of heaven Himself will prosper us; therefore we His servants will arise and build" (Nehemiah 2:20).

Third, we need persistence to overcome our failures and mistakes. Every person in pursuit of his goals and throughout their leadership will make mistakes and experience failures. The only one that does not make mistakes is the one that does nothing. We have demonstrated that everyone who has achieved success has experienced failures, but they have persisted and have not let a disappointment turn them into a failure.

Persistence to achieve your dreams and goals will propel you to get up and try again. With persistence, the Wright brothers succeeded in achieving their dreams of creating a machine that defied the law of gravity, the airplane. Edison created the light bulb, Lincoln became president, Louis Pasteur created the vaccine, and Max Lucado became a "best-selling" author after his manuscripts were rejected more than 12 times by publishers.

Fourth, we need to persist in order to move to new levels in our project and our lives. All promotion requires perseverance. The patriarch Jacob wrestled with the angel of the Lord all night at Peniel. That was the night where Jacob snatched his destiny, his new level. He went from Jacob, the deceiver, to Israel, the prince of God, thus giving continuity to the promise God made to Abraham. Jacob spent the night wrestling with the angel, and clearly said, "I will not let You go unless You bless me!" (Gen. 32:26). The story goes that the petition, struggle, and tension lasted all night and at daybreak, the angel finally revealed his new name. Jacob could move to a new level of success in his project because he persisted. The people who are moving from strength to strength and glory to glory know that they have an appointment at Peniel; they know that persistence is the key to the success of their project.

Likewise, the persistence of Ruth moved her to success; she became the wife of Boaz. She persisted in the midst of poverty, shortage, amidst the bitterness of her mother-in-law, Naomi, of loneliness, of being foreigner and living in uncertainty. Because she did not give up, she snatched her blessing and her goals.

Fifth, you need to be persistent, if you want to grasp your harvest. The problem of many people is not the sowing, but the process of waiting for the manifestation of their harvest. Many give up before the latter rain arrives. They know how to flow with the early rain, but do not have the persistence to expect the latter rain, which is the one that guarantees a good harvest. Paul wrote in Galatians 6:9 that in due time we will reap if we faint not, that is, if we persist, if we do not give up.

The preacher said: "Cast your bread upon the waters, for you will find it after many days" (Ecclesiastes 11:1). Wait for your bread. Learn to watch and wait.

Sixth, you need persistence to propel your projects, because every project needs to be covered with prayer. One of the secrets of prayer is perseverance. If you want to receive answers to your prayers, you must be persistent. You have to prevail in prayer to see your answer manifested. I know the problem with many is their lack of prayer, but the other problem is their failure to prevail or persist in prayer. They pray but do not prevail in prayer until they see their answer.

Many of us, when we do not see the answers to our prayers with the speed we want, we surrender. It is not just that we stop and pray, but we also surrender our goals and our projects. Prayer takes time. Not all prayers will be answered with the same speed. There are prayers, which by their very importance, relevance, and impact will receive much opposition in the air to prevent their response from arriving. For this reason, it is important for the leader to prevail in prayer and vigil.

Large projects face strong opposition

Cindy Trimm says, in her book **The Art of War for Spiritual Battle: Essential tactics and strategies for spiritual warfare**, that persistence is a key element of the effective prayer.

> It is not always in Satan's interest to block prayers from coming to pass. If the devil did, you might just pray all the more determined. So what he would rather do is let you convince yourself that prayers should always be this easy, then you will never learn to persevere in it ... He doesn't mind letting a casual prayer through here and there, as long as it keeps you convinced that prayer is like a vending machine where you put in your faith, push a button, and immediately your answer pops

out. In fact, it probably gives him a laugh, because you jump up and down, he is already envisioning your doubts and discouragement when he later hinders something bigger you will pray for; for he knows you will give up short of seeing it manifested ... You see, what Satan really doesn't want is a persistent, methodical, importunistic believer who lives by prayer. He doesn't want someone who is disciplined and tenacious in prayer that once that person begins to pray, Satan knows, no matter how long he fights to delay the answer he has no hope of winning. [6]

I believe wholeheartedly that every leader must learn to persevere in prayer. Consider the following examples that show the results of the principle of persistence and prayer.

- The widow in Luke 18 and the unjust judge: She persisted in her prayer and in her request. Day after day, she received no for an answer, but she kept persisting until she exhausted the patience of the unjust judge, and he relented and did her justice (v.5).

- When Jesus passed by, Bartimaeus began to shout for Jesus to heal him, but his prayer was opposed. The people told him to shut up, but nonetheless Bartimaeus persisted in his prayer. The story says that he cried out all the louder. He kept asking and praying until Jesus tended to him (Luke 18:38-39).

- The man who went to the house of his friend at midnight to ask for bread for a visitor that had come to his house, despite a no response from his friend, kept persisting in prayer until he was given what asked (Luke 11:8).

Pastor Joel Osteen shared an experience about the power of persistence. [6] He says he decided to climb a mountain. After a while, he felt very tired, and had not yet reached the top. He paused for air, and there thought about turning back. At that moment, coming down from the mountaintop was an older gentleman, who said to him: "You are closer than you think." This encouraged him to persist, and in ten minutes he reached the top, he reached his goal. He was about to give up just when he was closest to his goal. Persistence made the difference.

As always, the more difficult the situation gets, the more tired we are and think we can bear no more and plan to give up, that is when we are closest to achieving our goals. The darkest moment of the night is closest to the arrival of a new day. We are closer than we think. Persistence is the key to not staying halfway up the mountain and instead conquering the summit. Decide to be a persistent person. Your project needs your perseverance: persist!

Notes

1) Oscar Diaz, El Poder de la Persistencia (The Power of Persistence), p. 1

2) Myles Munroe, Spirit of Leadership, p.263

3) John Maxwell, Dare to Dream ... Then Do It, p.112

4) Myles Munroe, Spirit of Leadership, p. 265-266

5) Myles Munroe, Spirit of Leadership, p. 264

6) Cindy Trim, The Art of War for Spiritual Battle: Essential tactics and strategies for spiritual warfare, p. 30-31

7) Joel Osteen, It's Your Time, p.3-5

Guiding Questions - Chapter Seven

1) Write the principle found in Galatians 6:9.

2) Discuss the various definitions of perseverance and persistence.

3) What nourishes persistence in a person? How do you apply this to yourself?

4) How will persistence help you carry out your project as it pertains to the time dimension? Explain: "Every major project will require time." Give an example.

5) How will persistence help you face opposition to your project? Explain: "Every great project will experience opposition." Give an example.

6) How will perseverance help the realization of your project when you make mistakes and experience failures? Give an example.

7) Explain the passage of Jacob and the angel at Peniel, and how perseverance was a key element for him to move to a new level. How was perseverance demonstrated in Ruth, the Moabite?

8) Explain how perseverance relates to the law of sowing and reaping. Comment on Galatians 6: 9 and Ecclesiastes 11:1.

9) Explain the relationship between prayer and perseverance. Use Luke 18. Explain the thesis Cindy Trimm has on the subject.

10) Do you consider yourself persistent? How has this lesson helped you to assess and value persistence? Have you made the necessary changes?

8TH PRINCIPLE: EVALUATION

*The principle that challenges you to
examine and improve yourself*

Search me, God, and know my heart;
test me and know my concerns. See if
there is any offensive way in me; lead me
in the everlasting way.
Psalm 139:23-24

E valuation is the eighth powerful principle that will help propel your project. Evaluation is the art or the ability to exercise judgment about something. One of the many skills that human beings possess is the ability to assess, judge, and weigh not just what they do but also themselves. However, despite having this capacity, and the many benefits the assessment process renders, there are few who apply this capacity in a systematic way. For many, the process of evaluation can be threatening, because it brings forward information they do not want to hear or deal with. The evaluation can become a very tense confrontation, as it challenges you to accept responsibility and take positions on the facts received. You have to understand that if you want to succeed and grow, you need to go through the evaluation process. Not everything will be easy and enjoyable in life.

It is important to clarify that the evaluation process will show things that are not working, but it will also show what you are doing well and should affirm. What is the point of continuing to do those things that do not work? What good is it, if it does not have a positive effect on your goals? Why perpetuate strategies, habits, patterns, and procedures that are not producing as expected?

The principle of the evaluation must be an integral part of your life and your plan of action. It is not just for the critical times. If you want your project to progress daily, the evaluation should be performed periodically throughout the year. You must identify at least three valid sources for the evaluation: an internal source, an external source, and a source from above.

Internal evaluation source: Self-Evaluation

The first person that needs to be committed to the evaluation of yourself and your project is you. The other sources of evaluation should be supplemented with your own evaluation. To have an effective self-evaluation, you must commit to be honest and not deceive yourself. There is no worse deception than self-deception, or to believe the lies that are told to others. We tend to see very clearly the speck in the eyes of others, but we find it very difficult to see the log that is in our eyes. We are experts in judging, criticizing, and pointing out the faults of others, but we are exceedingly timid in dealing with our own. If our neighbor has some extra pounds, we call them fat, but if it is us, then they are healthy pounds. If a coworker is preferred by the boss, we quickly attribute it to their excessive efforts to curry favor, but if it is us, then we say that we have favor and grace.

The truth is that to have an efficient self-evaluation, you must have an adequate concept of yourself, and a good self-esteem. An adequate concept is neither about believing that you are all that and a bag of chips, nor that you are a filthy rag. The point is that you do not go around blaming yourself for everything and that due to a false sense of humility you fail to recognize the things you are doing well. There are people that live with a strong belief that they are not that good, that they have no value, and that nothing they do will work out. They live expecting their failure. A self-assessment with such a low perspective will not yield an accurate and fair evaluation.

A good example of a self-evaluation is found in the story of the prodigal son (Luke 15:17-19). The young man had the courage to re-examine his life and what was happening, in the light of his decisions. His self-assessment was a key element in his restoration and success. In the midst of his crisis, when he arrives at the very bottom, he decides to evaluate: how he was, where he was, why he was in that condition, what options he had and what he had to do.

He assessed his condition, "I perish here with hunger." He assessed the condition of his father's house where there was bread enough and to spare. He evaluated the cause of his failure: I have sinned; I recognize that my bad decisions are to blame for my condition.

With this assessment he then decided:

- I will arise.
- Return to the house of my father.
- I will go in an attitude of repentance and ask forgiveness.
- I will begin my life again in the house of my father, from the ground up starting as a hired servant.

Look at the power of a good self-evaluation. By accepting responsibility and not looking for someone to blame, he was able to assume an attitude of repentance, seek forgiveness, and leave behind his arrogant attitude.

External source of evaluation (the outsider)

Any balanced assessment counts on an external evaluation, in addition to an internal evaluation. You not only need to consider how you see yourself, but how others see you. This process is called feedback. The external evaluation is more threatening than the self-evaluation, but you need to know how other people perceive you. You need to know, because you may believe you are doing great work, and really, you are making a fool out of yourself. On the other hand, you might be thinking that what you are doing is small or irrelevant, when you are actually doing something of great impact in the eyes of others. If you know how others see you, you can make adjustments for the better.

Things look different depending on the angle or perspective from where they are looked at and on who is doing the looking. Sometimes you are "so close to yourself," that your view is distorted and you cannot see what is obvious to everyone. To obtain the best results, you must understand some basic rules of feedback. First, you cannot fall into the temptation of wanting to please everyone. Second, you cannot try to be as others want you to be. It is impossible to please or satisfy everyone. You cannot go by every corner asking: Do you like my hair? How can it be better? What color should I paint my living room? Do you like my new friend? No, is not about that. That would instead reflect insecurity. Feedback is not an order or command. What others share with you is only their perception; then it will be up to you to clarify, evaluate and give the necessary importance and weight to that perception.

Not everyone is qualified to give effective feedback. Unqualified people who envy or abhor you, who have declared themselves your enemy are not deserving of your time such that you would sit with and open your heart to them. Imagine if Nehemiah had invited Sanballat to ask him for an assessment or feedback about his calling and about the quality of the walls being erected. As it were, Sanballat, Geshem, and Tobias were giving Nehemiah a free evaluation, without being asked, but it was one that was contaminated, because they disagreed with the Nehemiah's project. The goal of Sanballat, Tobias, and Geshem in giving their evaluation of the quality of the work the Jewish people were doing was not to help them improve but rather to discourage them so they would end the project (see Nehemiah 4:1-3). That said, it's good to keep in mind that sometimes even your enemies, without it being their intention, can give you good feedback and help you improve. Be on your guard!

Throughout the construction of your project and your life, you should have key people around you that you trust, that are qualified, that love and respect you, but that also have the space to tell you how they see you in both the good and in the areas that need improvement. Spouses, parents, children, friends, mentors, and spiritual leaders fall into that category. These people, even if they are wrong in their assessment, have no hidden agenda, because they love you, want what is best for you, and want you to do well. It is good to listen to them.

Jethro, the father-in-law of Moses, is a positive example of an external evaluation. He loved Moses, recognized his leadership position, respected him, and had no hidden agenda. From the outside, he could see what Moses was doing to solve people's problems from morning until evening. Jethro could look ahead and see the negative results that Moses and the people would receive if changes were not made. Moses was giving himself wholeheartedly. He was devoting all of his efforts and time as a responsible leader, but Jethro says: "The thing that you do is not good. Both you and these people who are with you will surely wear yourselves out." (see Exodus 18:13-23). Look at the style used by Jethro to provide feedback: first, he talks to Moses alone, and gives his assessment and advice with respect. Second, he does not try to impose himself, but rather brings forward his evaluation, only as an exchange of information to shed light on the situation. Third, he lets Moses make the ultimately decision of what to do about it.

Moses appreciated the effort of his father-in-law. He took time to hear and appreciate what Jethro said about his efforts and performance. We do not see Moses on the defensive, not resorting to his title or position as leader over his father-in-law. Moses was God's anointed, with firsthand terrifying experiences with God, but was now receiving an evaluation from his father-in-law, who came from a pagan background. Moses was humble and simple enough to receive the suggestions. He did not claim that he knew it all, and that he was perfect; he did not let title or position get to his head. You need to know that you can learn even from a child. Do not despise anyone's advice or evaluation.

Moses then sought for 70 elderly people of integrity and experience to assist him in his efforts. Once he entrusted them to do the work his load was most certainly lightened. He succeeded, thanks to an external evaluation from an outsider who saw him in action and gave wise advice for his benefit and improvement. Do not be afraid to submit yourself to the scrutiny or evaluation of others, because you may receive the best counsel of your life to propel your project and help you succeed. Have you already identified people who can evaluate you? When are you going to make an appointment with them to start the process?

Evaluation source from above (God)

The third effective source for help in the evaluation process is God himself. Your creator and loving Father provides the assessment that comes from above. In Psalm 139:23-24, David makes an unusual prayer, because what he is asking of God is not material, financial, or physical. David is asking God himself to evaluate him. He says: examine, test, and know me and see if there is any wicked way in me. He is saying, give me an assessment of how am doing and at what level I am. It is a challenging prayer.

David asks for that assessment, because his goal was to continue advancing in the everlasting way. David desires the perfect plan for his life, with all of his heart. He does not want to delay, but rather to move his project forward. Therefore, he asks God to look him over from top to bottom, inside and out, without restrictions or secret areas. David wanted God to seek those things he had inside, and could be negatively affecting his progress. This point is important: the evaluation process will make sense only for those people who have goals and want to meet them. If you have no goals or projects, you will be indifferent from one thing and the other, and the evaluation would be a waste of time and effort.

David understood that no one knew him better than God, that no one loved him more than God, and nobody wanted what was best for him more than God did. For that reason he did not want to leave God out of his gaze. David had no suspicion or distrust of God, and he was even less afraid.

79

Perfect love casts out fear (1 John 4:18). He knew he could fully rely on God; that God was not a gossip or a person who would enjoy seeing his faults so he could discredit and destroy him. What a beautiful relationship David had with his creator!

Now I ask you: what is your relationship with God? How do you see God? How important and decisive is God's opinion to you? Do you trust in him? Do you keep secret areas or facades for God? Can you make of your heart the prayer that David made?

It is worthwhile to have God in your evaluation team, to count with his perspective, and what he has to say to you. If you have God's opinion, nothing can prevent your blessing. Through the study of the Word, intimate prayer and the ministering of the Holy Spirit, God will let you know, like he did David, those things that are on your way, that arrest your progress or even bring harm to you. You will also know what things are for your good, what things you need, and what things you should retain. Definitely, all of this will propel you on your everlasting way. Nothing is more helpful than to set aside every so often, days of spiritual retreat, of prayer, fasting and solitude, to give the Lord a chance to evaluate, examine, test and know you. With the result of that spiritual exploration you can move forward confident in your project. The benefit will be immense.

Your project needs the principle of the evaluation. It would be powerful, if you could now pray like David and say,

"Search me, O God, and know my heart; Try me, and know my anxieties; and see if there is any wicked way in me, and lead me in the way everlasting."

Psalm 139:23-24

Amen.

Guiding Questions - Chapter Eight

1) Why can the evaluation process be threatening for many people?

2) Why are evaluations critical to the progress of our lives and our projects?

3) Why do you think the author says that the evaluation should occur not only during the critical times, but also as a regular part of our lives? Use the examples of the annual medical exam and the maintenance checks done on cars every three thousand miles.

4) Is the evaluation process a systematic part of your life and your projects? If not, why?

5) What are the three sources mentioned by the author to help in a good evaluation?

6) What criteria should be taken into account when we do a self-evaluation? Explain the self-evaluation of the prodigal son. What did you learn?

7) Why is an external evaluation important? What rules must be taken into account here? Share what affected you the most of the Jethro's assessment of Moses, and the relationship and exchange between them. What did you learn?

8) Why is God's evaluation so important?

9) Why did David yearn for a divine evaluation? Do you?

10) Why was David not scared of an evaluation from God? What was his relationship to God? How did this relationship help with the divine evaluation? What is your relationship with God? Can you pray with total confidence and sincerity as David did in Psalm 139:23-24?

BIBLIOGRAPHY

Diaz, Oscar, **El Poder de la Persistencia (The Power of Persistence)**, Editorial Renovación, Springfield, MA 2008.

Dollar, Creflo, **8 Steps to Create the Life You Want: The Anatomy of a Successful Life**, FaithWords, Nashville, TN, 2008.

Jakes, TD **Before You Do: Making Great Decisions That You Won't Regret**, Publisher Atria Books, NY, NY, 2008.

Maxwell, John, **The choice is yours,** Macmillan, Nashville, TN, 2005.

Maxwell, John, **Dare to Dream ... Then Do It,** Thomas Nelson Inc., Nashville, TN, 2006

Morris, Robert, **The Power of Your Words,** Regal Books, Ventura, CA, 2006.

Moya, Tommy, **Destined for heights**, Creation House, Lake Mary, Florida, 2005.

Munroe, Myles, **Spirit of Leadership,** Whitaker House, Philadelphia, 2005.

Murdock, Mike, **The Law of Recognition**, Wisdom International, Dallas, Texas, 1999.

Murdock, Mike, **The Uncommon Dream,** Wisdom International, Fort Worth, Texas, 2006.

Muratori, John, **Rich Church Poor Church: Unlock the Secrets of Creating Wealth and Harness the Power of Money to Influence Everything**, GateKeeper Publishing, Cheshire, CT, 2007.

Newberry, Tommy, **Success Is Not an Accident: Change Your Choices; Change Your Life**, Tyndale House, Carol Stream, Illinois, 2007.

Osorio, Rafael, **Moving to a New Level: Unleashing God's Purpose for Your Life,** Editorial Renovación, Springfield, MA, 2009.

Osteen, Joel, **It's Your Time,** Free Press, New York, 2009

Trimm, Cindy, **The Art of War for Spiritual Battle: Essential tactics and strategies for spiritual warfare**, Creation House, Florida, 2010.

Wagner, Peter C., **Dominion,** Chosen Books, Michigan, 2008.

www.ingramcontent.com/pod-product-compliance
Lightning Source LLC
Chambersburg PA
CBHW031327040426
42443CB00005B/249